EVEN THE TREES DO IT

YVONNE DAVIS-WEIR

Foreword written by my daughters
Samantha Spann and Sasha Saunders.

WESTBOW
PRESS®
A DIVISION OF THOMAS NELSON
& ZONDERVAN

WestBow Press books may be ordered through booksellers or by contacting:

WestBow Press
A Division of Thomas Nelson & Zondervan
1663 Liberty Drive
Bloomington, IN 47403
www.westbowpress.com
844-714-3454

ISBN: 978-1-6642-9158-4 (sc)
ISBN: 978-1-6642-9160-7 (hc)
ISBN: 978-1-6642-9159-1 (e)

Library of Congress Control Number: 2023902130

Print information available on the last page.

WestBow Press rev. date: 6/26/2023

I dedicate this book to the
memory of my first-born
son Michael Stanley
October 8, 1976 –
December 26, 2019

Rest in Peace, my son.

PREFACE

Have you ever wondered why we were so lovingly and beautifully created? Why our Creator made such a beautiful world with everything in it to sustain us? I believe He created us to worship Him wholeheartedly. He didn't create us and left us to fend for ourselves, He was certain to include everything that we would need to sustain us throughout our lives. He made certain that we would not lack anything, He did these things for us in such a way that we will be able to make allowance to worship. That's the kind of God we serve, One who loves us unconditionally, and One who always completes what He started. Therefore it is our duty to be obedient, and to worship. Our days should be filled with praise and worship to our Lord, Savior and Creator. This should not be an issue as far as glorifying Him is concerned, because He made everything for our comfort. therefore nothing should prevent us from giving Him His due.

As Christians, we must develop an attitude of praise so that eventually, it will happen naturally. For me, I realize that when I stay in praise and worship-mode, I get to enjoy my days in peace. I am by no means saying that I don't have problems, or run into difficult situations sometimes; I am saying that when I delight myself in my Savior, my problems are more bearable and easier to manage. I am able to think, plan and act as the Holy Spirit leads me. Thinking and doing things on my own usually leads to problems which are costly to me in every way. Sometimes when I attempt to do it on my own, my problems would appear to be solved, but only to realize later that the solution was only temporary. From the many mistakes I've made over the years, I began to realize that trying to do it without God is not the way, it will certainly lead to destruction. So, it's important for us to adopt a lifestyle of praise and worship, lean on God for strength, look to Him for guidance, and I guarantee that we will see positive results. And in those cases where you don't see results, it doesn't mean that God has abandoned you, He is in fact working on your behalf. In the meantime He will provide that peace which will sustain you throughout. The scripture is constantly reminding us to keep on trusting in Him. One of those is found in Proverbs which states "Trust in the Lord with all your heart. And lean not on your own understanding; In all your ways acknowledge Him, And He shall direct your paths" (NKJV).

FOREWORD

SAMANTHA N. SPANN

When we think of praising God, we often picture Sunday morning worship services. We also sometimes think of praise only happening during the praise and worship part of the service. Through this book, it broadens our understanding of what praise is and what it can look like in our day to day living.

"Even the Trees do it" explores the importance of praise and how it can transform our relationship with God.

FOREWORD

SASHA E. SAUNDERS

"Let everything that hath
breath, praise the Lord!
Praise ye the Lord!"

Mom has always felt a responsibility to let the breath in her lungs be used to honor, lift up, and make known the power and love of God. Throughout her years and various experiences, she has held true to that one inner desire: to speak good of the name of Jesus, her personal Savior and confidant.

I love the way my mother, Yvonne Davis-Weir, fully and completely loves God and entirely trusts His word and His leadership. Her faith in His ability to provide for and work every situation for "good" is pure and motivating. Her devotion inspires the hearts of those she encounters, and she speaks good every chance she gets. I am proud of my mom and her persistence in being the best version of herself in this world. I admire her openness to learn, and the grace in which she exudes while learning. I respect her views and love how she is driven to serve and help others to move forward in their lives.

Mommy's passion to praise God was instilled in her from her parents and burns brightly within my own soul. I am reminded when mom speaks of the beauty, and love, and worthiness of God, and it humbles me and reminds me to never take the breath in my lungs for granted. The wind, the rain; the sunshine, the trees … they all reflect the artistry of our Creator. I live to also offer praise and honor and respect to God.

I love you, mommy, and am ever proud of the way you have surmounted life's obstacles to offer your writing as love notes to all. I hope and pray that those who read your words feel your passion and answer the call to praise!

Love,

Sasha

MY PRAYER OF
THANKSGIVING

Father in heaven, I love You so much. I am so grateful to You for loving me back, even though I am undeserving of Your love. Thank You for rescuing me from the path of destruction, and placing me in the right direction. Without Your unconditional love for me Lord, I don't know where I would be right now. Because You saved me, Lord, my desire is to praise and worship You for as long as I have breath. I am a praiser and a worshipper because doing so help me to get through each day whether my day is good or bad. My prayer is that this book will teach Your people about the importance of praise, and how effective it can be especially in turbulent as well as good times. My determination is to praise You every day of my life, and I look forward to continued praising and worshiping You with the angels in heaven. I thank You for giving me this great desire to praise You. It has strengthened me in my every-day walk and I am always grateful. I give You thanks for the wisdom to write every word in this book, and I thank You for choosing and using me to do Your will. I love, worship and adore You Father. Thank You for giving me daily strength. I pray this in Your most holy name, amen.

CONTENTS

ACKNOWLEDGEMENT

First, I give all honor and glory to God, the Creator of heaven and earth.

I dedicate this book to my parents Melbourne and Edith Davis, who spent their lives raising my sisters and myself knowing and understanding the value of true praise and worship.

Also to my children Michael (deceased), Linval, Sasha, Carlton Jr., Samantha and Clifford. The Lord could not have chosen a better, caring, loving and more understanding group. I feel so honored to be chosen to be their mom. I am also honored to be chosen as a daughter to my wonderful parents.

I acknowledge my professors both past and present at Trinity International and Liberty Universities. I thank them for helping me to expose the gifts God placed in me that I never knew existed. I appreciate their contribution very much.

I also appreciate the prayers and positive contributions from my family and friends on Facebook and Instagram. I thank them for always including me in their prayers.

To my church family at Lighthouse Christian Fellowship, you are amazing and I love you very much. Thank you for covering me with your prayers

Last but not least, my wonderful and supportive family at work (CIS Christian School). They help to make my days bearable. We share our good and bad days together and we always bounce back, preparing for the challenges of the next day.

ONE

ALL PRAISE IS DUE TO HIM

"Let everything that hath breath praise the Lord." Psalm 150:6. KJV.

ISN'T IT AMAZING HOW OUR GRACIOUS GOD so lovingly, wonderfully and carefully created us in His image to live in, and to enjoy such a beautiful world? A world that has everything, down to the smallest detail, for our comfort? He took great pride in creating us and He positioned us here and gave us dominion over the earth, to 'rule over the fish in the sea and the birds in the sky, over the livestock and all the wild animals and over all the creatures that move along the ground.' (Genesis 1:26, NIV). In addition to our responsibilities as caretakers, the Holy One also expects us to worship Him wholeheartedly. Since we will be joining the angels in heaven in worshipping our Lord and Savior at the end of our earthly journey, what better way and place to practice than to include worship in our daily lives while here on earth? John MacArthur says "Worship is our innermost being responding with praise for all that God is, through our attitudes, actions, thoughts, and words, based on the truth of God as He revealed Himself."[1]

As the One who sees and knows all, He knew beforehand that there would be times when we would become rebellious and refuse to give Him praise for various reasons. Some are currently experiencing broken hearts, broken homes, and brokenness from every angle. Some are suffering from different forms of sicknesses and diseases. Some have watched their loved ones suffer horribly and died as a result. Many of us sit at the bedside of loved ones and watched

[1] John MacArthur. Ultimate Priority. Moody Press

them breathe their last breath. These, and many other happenings make us so tired and beaten, many have become so discouraged that they even refuse to go to church because they don't feel the need to offer praise to God.

What we fail to understand is that when we praise God, it helps to lighten our loads, and takes our minds off our problems, and on to God. Another fact we fail to understand is that once we enter into the house of God, we are clearly sending a message to the devil. He hates God and His children so much that he will stop at nothing to keep us from praising and worshipping. 2 Corinthians 11:3 states "But I am afraid that just as Eve was deceived by the serpent's cunning, your minds may somehow be led astray from your sincere and pure devotion to Christ" (NIV). There was a story in the Bible where a couple (Ananias and Sapphira) were caught robbing God. The husband paid with his life. A similar fate happened to his wife. Then Peter said 'Ananias, how is it that Satan has so filled your heartbeat you have lied to the Holy Spirit and have kept for yourself some of the money you received for the land?' (Acts 5:3, NIV). Verse 10 further states "At that moment she fell down at his feet and died. Then the young man came in and, finding her dead, carried her out and buried her beside her husband" (NIV). If we permit him, the devil will do everything in his power to lure us into his traps by causing us to fall into sin. A word of caution from 1 Peter 5:8 and 9 "Be sober, be vigilant, because your adversary the devil, as a roaring lion, wanders about, seeking whom he may devour" (KJV).

Therefore, in spite of what we're experiencing in our lives, we must understand that no matter how educated or wealthy we are, when trouble comes, those resources cannot help us; we need Jesus to help us through. However, sometimes God allows some things to happen to us in order to make us better Christians. 1 Peter 1:7 says "That the trial of your faith, being much more precious than of gold that perisheth, though it be tried with fire, might be found unto praise and honor and glory at the appearing of Jesus Christ"(KJV).

Giving praise and thanks to our Lord and Savior should come to us naturally, especially since He has always been good to us. However, in spite of His grace towards us, there are many who either choose to praise God, or totally refuse to praise. Therefore, He created everything that is needed for us to praise Him, and He said "Let everything that hath breath praise the Lord" (KJV). When He said 'everything' He meant everything. He also meant that our praise and worship must be done all the time, this includes good times as well as bad times, when we feel like worshipping as well as when we don't feel like worshipping, whenever we have money and whether our finances are low. Whatever is going on in our lives, we must serve the Lord at all times, in spite of. This is important because everything (and I mean everything) we have are gifts from Him, even our lives are from God. So, since He gives us everything for our well-being and our comfort, the only wise thing to do is to give Him thanks. And what better way to thank and praise Him than through our worship? According to Charles Spurgeon

> In Christ, we have always been preserved
> by the power of God, always been secure
> of the heritage given to us in covenant
> by the blood of Christ; therefore, let us

always be grateful. If we are not always
singing with our lips, let us always be
singing with our hearts[2]

We must remember that all the money that we own
is of no use to Him. I am thankful for that because
if our monetary standing was a requirement to get
into heaven, many (including myself) would lose that
opportunity. Our gracious God has made it so easy
for us to serve Him, it does not cause a cent, yet we
make it so difficult to grant Him what He requested.

Many of us praise God only when things are going well
for us; when the bills are paid, food is in abundance,
the dog is fed, and everyone is happy, those are the
times we give God a high-five every now and then
because things are 'good.' During these times we are
so pleased with how God is running the show that
we sometimes will look up to heaven and say 'You're
the man, God. Good work' But how do we handle
ourselves when trouble comes? when everything
seems to be going anyway but good, when the bills
are pilling up and food is scarce? How do we see God

---

[2] Charles Spurgeon. The Power of Praising God. Whitaker House.

then? Is He still good? Will we still be praising Him like we did before?

God wants us to have the mentality that even if things do not go our way, even if the bank account is negative and the bills are overdue, He is still good and He is still God. He wants us to praise Him every hour of the day, in good or bad times, happy or sad times, or whether we have or have not. He wants us to be continuous and sincere in our praise the same way He is ceaseless and uninterrupted in His love for us. Our wishy-washy and namby-pamby ways of praising just won't do, and is totally unacceptable.

TWO

HOW DO WE PRAISE GOD?

WE CAN PRAISE GOD IN SO MANY WAYS, AND THE benefits will be just as rewarding. The most important thing is to ensure that our hearts are into our praise, because at the end of the day that's all that matters. The church doesn't have to be huge and decorated with wall-to-wall carpeting, expensive furniture, and the lighting doesn't have to be right. It doesn't matter who is staring at us, or who is whispering behind our backs. Being one with God is most important. When our praise is just a show for the onlookers, or if there are other selfish motives, then God is not involved and He's certainly not getting the glory. Look at the story of the different worship styles of Old Testament brothers Cain and Abel. The Bible said that,

> In the course of time Cain brought some of the fruits of the soil as an offering to the Lord. And Abel also brought an offering – fat portions from some of the firstborn of his flock. The Lord looked with favor on Abel and his offering, but on Cain and his offering he did not look with favor. So Cain was very angry and his face was downcast" (Genesis 4:3-5, NIV).

Our sincere praise can make a world of difference. It is very important that our focus is directly set on God during our praise and worship. These are some of the many ways that we can praise and worship God passionately. In Amos 5:21-24 the Lord states.

I hate, I despise your feast days, and I will not smell in your solemn assemblies. Though ye offer me burnt offerings and your meat offerings, I will not accept them, neither will I regard the pace offerings of your fat beasts. Take thou away from me the noise of thy songs: for I will not hear the melody of thy viols. But let judgement run down as waters, and righteousness as a mighty stream (KJV). Our God is a god of love and order. He accepts our praise and worship, but it must be sincere. In order words: it must come from the heart. In this instance, the people's praise was wonderful, they did the right thing and said the right words. However, one thing was missing: their sincerity. They were giving God only lip service, noting was coming from their hearts. So, He used Amos to warn them of their evil ways. This why Cain's worship to God was rejected.

Here are some of the many ways that we can praise God:

We can praise God with our words

One important fact, lest we forget, is that our words have power. Therefore we must be careful how we use them, because the results can be devastating. Moreover they are indications of what we are thinking. Proverbs 18:21 states "The tongue has the power of life and death, and those who love it will eat its fruit" (NIV).

In fact there is a biblical story about Joshua and his followers who used their words of praise to bring down the walls of Jericho. The Canaanites, because of their wickedness and stubbornness, were about to be severely punished by God, for their disobedience. Joshua was instructed to march with his people around the city of Jericho for seven days. On the seventh day they were told to repeat the march seven times. Upon the seventh day, the people praised, worshipped with their instruments. Joshua 6:20-21 say "When the trumpets sounded, the army shouted, and at the sound of the trumpet, when the men gave a loud shout, the wall collapsed; so everyone charged straight in it – men and women, young and old, sheep and donkeys" (NIV).

One thing about praising God vocally is that we can never be at a loss for words. In case we don't know what to say or how to express ourselves, we certainly can go to the Holy Bible. In addition to its great teaching, this amazing Book also teaches us how to worship. In fact one of the many true worshippers mentioned in Bible times was King David, a 'man after God's own heart.' (Acts 13:22).

David may not be the best, he may not have been the most ethical king; and he may not have had what it took to receive the "Parent of the Year" award, but he certainly knew how to praise God. His words of praise are evident in many of the Psalms which we still find useful today as we go through our daily struggles. As we endure our struggles and as we read King David's Psalms, we tend to have a better understanding of what he was going through. We also learn how his songs of praise and worship helped him to endure his many trials.

Psalms 103:1-3 say "Praise the Lord, my soul; all my inmost being, praise his holy name. Praise the Lord, my soul, and forget not all his benefits - who forgives all your sins and heals all your diseases, who redeems your life from the pit and crowns you with love and compassion, who satisfies your desires with good things so that your youth is renewed like the eagle's" (NIV).

Psalm 111:1 states "I will extol the Lord with all my heart in the council of the upright and in the assembly" (NIV).

Psalm 9:2-3 say "I will be glad and rejoice in you; I will sing the praises of your name, O Most High. My enemies turn back; they stumble and perish before you" (NIV).

The psalmist also say in Psalm 34: 2-4 "My soul shall make her boast in the Lord: the humble shall hear thereof and be glad. O magnify the Lord with me, and let us exalt his name together. I sought the Lord, and he heard me, and delivered me from all my fears" (KJV).

David had that crazy way of praising and worshipping, this is evident in the time of his son's death. For those of us who experienced the death of a loved one, we are so deep into our sadness that worshipping is the last thing on our minds. While writing this book, my oldest son went home to be with the Lord. It put me in another way of thinking and all the things I would normally do were put on hold. Praising and worshipping were secondary because I was in so much pain. Yet this man of God, this great worshipper rose up after his son's death, and worshipped the Lord. 2 Samuel 12:16 say "David therefore sought God on behalf of the child" Verse 18 says "On the seventh day the child died" Verse 20 states "Then David rose from the earth and washed and anointed himself and changed his clothes. And he went into the house of the Lord and worshipped" (ESV).

The Bible also described King David during a happier time, dancing in the streets according to 2 Samuel 6:14. The scripture says "And David danced before the Lord with all his might; and David was girded with a linen ephod" (KJV). He danced so hard that it displeased his wife Michal (Saul's daughter). She said in 2 Samuel 6:20 "How glorious was the King of Israel today, who uncovered himself today in the eyes of the handmaids of his servants, as one of the vain fellows shamelessly uncovered himself" (KJV). Not everyone will understand your praise, David's wife certainly did not understand his. However we must continue to praise Him anyway.

2 Chronicles chapter 20 showed how Jehoshaphat praised God straight into victory during a very stressful time in his life. The Moabites, Ammonites and some other nations declared war on this man of God. Naturally many leaders would gather their armies together and prepare for battle. However, this

leader decided to go into praise-mode. Verse 9 says "If calamity comes upon us, whether the sword of judgement, or plaque or famine, we will stand in your presence before this temple that bears your Name and will cry out to you in our distress, and you will hear us and save us" (NIV).

These and many other biblical stories are clear indication that God hears us when we call upon Him through prayer, praise or worship. When we pray and cry out, shout out or sing to God Almighty, we are also in fact offering praise to Him. In verse 21 the story tells how this king glorified God with all his heart. "After consulting the people, Jehoshaphat appointed men to sing to the Lord and to praise him for the splendor of high holiness's they went out at the head of the army saying 'Give thanks to the Lord for his love endures forever" (NIV).

We can also praise Him in silence

For me, sometimes when I see the powerful ways in which God moves in my life, I am at a loss for words. The most amazing thing about my relationship with God is that words are not necessary sometimes, because

He understands me with or without words. So when my words fail me at times, I just sit in silence, and even in my silence, my heavenly Father understands me. Many people believe that if one's arms are not raised up in the air, and one is not being vocal in their praises, then it's not considered to be a form of praise. On many occasions when I am in church and I am moved by the Holy Spirit, I sometimes sit or stand in silence, with my eyes closed, And sometimes a bit teary-eyed

I vividly remember being called out of my seat while visiting a church. This was during praise and worship, and I remembered standing with my eyes closed. The moderator/pastor called me up to the front during praise-and-worship. As a pastor myself, I thought that she probably wanted me to pray before that segment of the service was concluded. However to my surprise, she ordered me to clap my hands and sing. She said she wanted to remind me of God's greatness for which I should be grateful. My moment of silent praise was interrupted and I no longer felt that feeling of reverence before God during the service. I thought briefly how much I was being judged by that individual, all because I chose to worship my God in a way that I was comfortable.

I am reminded of a story in Luke chapter 18:10-14

> Two men went up to the temple to pray, one a Pharisee and the other a tax collector. The Pharisee stood by himself and prayed: 'God, I thank you that I am not like these people – robbers, evildoers, adulterers – or even like this tax collector. I fast twice a week and give a tenth of all I get. But the tax collector stood at a distance. He would not even look up to heaven, but beat his breast and said, 'God, have mercy on me, a sinner' I tell you that this man, rather than the other, went home justified before God. For all those who exalt themselves will be humbled, and those who humble themselves will be exalted" (NIV).

There is nothing wrong with our silent praise, it is a dialogue between the individual and our Heavenly Father which no one else can understand. When this is happening, it is not for us to become critical and condemning. Praising God without words can be in the form of the raising of the hands, the bowing of the head, the clasping of the hands in reverence, standing, sitting or kneeling before the Lord. It is an individual experience which does not call for everyone to understand.

It is important for us to be comfortable with our praise, instead of worrying about how we will be perceived by others. 1 Samuel chapter 1 told a story about a woman named Hanna. She had a need and she went to the Lord with her request. She praised God in silence, and only God heard her request. The priest saw her in the temple silently praising God and misunderstood her actions as signs of drunkenness. Many times we will be misunderstood by the world, and as a result we will be judged wrongfully. However let us not allow that or anything to halt or limit our praise. At the end of the day, our sole intention is to praise God, and not man.

We can also praise God with our instruments

> **Shout for joy to the Lord, all the earth,**
> **burst into jubilant song with music;**
> **make music to the Lord with the**
> **harp, with the harp and the sound of**
> **singing, with trumpets and the blast of**
> **the ram's horn shout for joy before the**
> **Lord, the King. Psalm 98:4-6. NIV.**

There are clear biblical evidences that the use of musical instruments were encouraged and used during praise and worship.

"And he stationed the Levites in the house of the Lord with cymbals, harps, and lyres, according to the commandment of David and of God the king's seer and of Nathan the prophet, for the commandment was from the Lord through his prophets" 2 Chronicles 20:25. ESV. God, in His infinite wisdom created musical instruments, and He gave man the ability to use these instruments for His honor and glory. These instruments are being used both on earth and in heaven to glorify God. Revelation 14:2 says "And I heard a voice from heaven as the voice of many waters, and as the voice of a great thunder, and I heard the voice of harpers harping with their harps" (KJV).

Back to the story of King David, when it comes to praise and worship, he had no inhibitions, wherever and whenever, he was always prepared to glorify God. "David had no qualms about redeeming these musical instruments for their true purpose of glorifying God." [3]

According to Exodus 15:20-21

> And Miriam the prophetess, the sister of Aaron, took a timbrel in her hand; and all the women went out after her with timbrels and with dances. And Miriam answered them, Sing ye to the Lord, for he hath triumphed gloriously; the horse and his rider hath he thrown into the sea (KJV).

After all, Miriam just couldn't help herself, she had just witnessed something beyond spectacular. She had proven God's faithfulness towards His people once more. She watched how God used Moses to part the Red Sea in order to allow His people to escape the wrath of Pharaoh and his men. She also saw how God allowed the water to swallow up and destroyed

---

[3] John Dickson & Chuck D. Pierce. Chosen Books. Bloomington, MN.

all the men who were trying to harm the Israelites. Witnessing something so impressive and memorable certainly is cause for praise and worship. This was not the only time that the Israelites offer praise to God, "Instruments of music were employed by the Israelites in the praises of God, from the time of their departure out of the land of Egypt." [4]

Similarly, instruments were used in Bible times and in heaven to enhance the praise and worship. These instruments were created by God, for God.

We praise God while fellowshipping with others

Let the message of Christ dwell among you richly as you teach and admonish one another with all wisdom through psalms, hymns, and songs from the Spirit, singing to God with gratitude in your hearts. Colossians 3:16. NIV.

As believers in Jesus Christ we need each other,

---

[4] James Begg. The Use of Instruments of Music. Puritan Publications. Coconut Creek, FL.

especially living in a world that is saturated with corruption, violence and hate. A world where sin and evil have taken up permanent residency in our homes, and are targeting God's people minute by minute. Therefore, we need to be in constant fellowship, and remain close to one another in order to be spiritually strong and alert. There is strength in numbers, and when we bind ourselves together in God's love, much can be accomplished. Christian fellowship is very important in our spiritual journey. It goes way beyond meeting in church on our day of worship. It involves keeping each other accountable at all times, praying, and covering each other through prayer and fasting. This fellowship with each other, must go beyond working capacity, it's for leisure-time as well. According to Dr. Curry,[5]

> Many christians underestimate Satan, meaning that we sometimes take salvation for granted, gets laid back thinking that we have all the answers and then we let our guards down and the enemy comes

---

[5] Curry Sr, Rickey L., How to stay focused on a christian journey, Advanced Global Publishing. Shippensburg, PA.

in to rob us of the joy that Jesus Christ has given us through the Holy Spirit. We have to continue serving God in and out of season meaning that we have to pray when we feel like praying, and pray when we don't feel like praying. Continuous service to the Lord becomes a part of our lives, and then it will not so easy for Satan to infiltrate the lives of Christian and any delivers of potential believers (Curry Sr. 2014).

Hebrews 10:24-25 say "And let us consider how to stir up one another in love and good works, not neglecting to meet together, as is the habit of some, but encouraging one another, and all the more as you see the Day drawing near" (ESV).

We cannot forget the important fact that Jesus is also a worshipper. There are biblical evidences that He praised the Father with His disciples, and He sometimes did it alone. In Matthew 26 after Holy Communion, verse 30 states "When they had sung a hymn, they went out to the Mount of Olives" (NIV). Also in Hebrews 2:12 Jesus publicly declared that "I will declare your name to my brothers and sisters; in the assembly I will sing your praises" (NIV). In His final hours on earth Jesus reached out to His Heavenly Father in praise "After Jesus said this, he looked toward heaven and prayed; 'Father, the hour has come. Glorify your son, that your Son may glorify you" (John 17:1. NIV).

It is vital for like-minded people to come together as one, to worship. Acts chapter 2 describes the disciples worshipping together, and more importantly, they were all on one accord. Verse 1 states "When the day of Pentecost came, they were all together in one place" (NIV). The Holy Spirit was able to operate effectively because there was no discord among them, they were all on one accord. I conducted many interviews prior to writing this book, and was astonished to discover that many people believe that they don't need to come together with others in the church in order to have true unity in worship. Of course, they offered several reasons why they refuse to do so. However, if one is sharing the same faith in God with others, then they need to be in fellowship with one another. In John 17:20-22 Jesus prayed for unity,

> My prayer is not for them alone. I pray also for those who will believe in me through their message, that all of them may be one. Father, just as you are in me and I am in you. May they also be in us so that the world may believe that you have sent me. I have given them the glory that you gave me, that they may be one as we are one (NIV).

Christians coming together in love and unity send a very clear message to the world. It is also sending an invitation for others to come and join. When the world sees that we are unified and strengthened in genuine love, chances are that they will have the desire to partake.

> Pleasing worship of God is done mainly in two ways, in song and in prayer. In song worship usually is done with music while singing from the heart with others, for God inhabits our praise. In prayer it is done best by quietly talking to Him

while alone and under the Holy Spirit's inspirational direction.[6]

We also praise God in our pain.

I would like to pray this prayer before I proceed.

Father, as I go through the valley right now, I ask for strength and every kind of reinforcement that I will need to go through this process. It is during this time of great pain when Your people sometimes become vulnerable, times when the devil is more likely to present himself and attempt to lure us away from You. So, I am asking You Father to be my strength during my time of pain. Help me to understand that there is nothing that Your children endure that You haven't endured. You experienced the loss of Your only

[6] William H. Mulder. Fellowship with God in Spirit & Truth. Xulon Press. Maitland, FL.

Son, You've endured great pain, so You understand. Anoint Your servant afresh each day Lord as I go through the valley. Amen.

I was almost close to finish writing this book when my firstborn son Michael passed away. So I decided to add this section to my writing. The fact that I am going through so much right now, I decided to put a hold on completing this book, nevertheless, I am feeling that sense of urgency to continue. I think it not strange or coincidental that at this time of grieving, I am writing a book about praise and worship. I know that it was God's will for me to do this at this time, and I must be obedient to His words, and continue. I believe that God provided a way for me to describe what I am going through. Otherwise I would not have been able to pen my feelings and experiences during this very difficult time. I learned how distressing, tough and hard it can be when one loses a child and the indescribable pain that is attached to it. I also learn how to hold on to God for strength and support. Singing many encouraging hymns in church, in the past. Now I realize how meaningful and comforting the words of those songs can be. As one songwriter Barney E. Warren says "Farther along we'll know more about it, Farther along we'll understand why; Cheer up, my brother, live in the sunshine, We'll understand it all by and by" There are so many things that we don't understand, however we must cheer up, and be encouraged knowing that God is always with us, and is always in control.

It has been two days since the tragedy and I am in so much pain. This type of pain cannot be alleviated by any form of medication, and it cannot be described. I need to feel God's presence around me at ALL times. So I resort to praising God by thanking Him for holding me. Prayers are so effective, and with loved ones praying for me, I can feel the effects. Each time I am about to fall apart, I can feel the Holy Spirit lifting me and holding me up. I am weak from crying constantly but I can feel the divine help from above. The experience is so surreal, but in a good, peaceful way. I know that I am going through, but I am encouraged in knowing that I am not alone. When we're dealing with issues beyond our control, when life seems unbearable, we need to remember God's undying and unchanging love for us. That is the only way that we can endure our pain. "David proclaimed his deep yearning for God as he hid from his enemies in the desert. Remembering his personal encounters with God's limitless power and satisfying love led him to praise. Through his most difficult nights, David could still rejoice in his dependable Father's loving care." [7] Now I see the importance of praising God in the midst of my pain. I am speaking this from experience, and I am very happy to tell everyone that God is real, He is loving and sincere. When He says He is with us, He is with us.

In addition to my wonderful experiences with Him, I am basking in the words of His unbroken promises: Joshua 1:9 "Have I not commanded you? Be strong and courageous. Do not be frightened, and do not be dismayed, for the Lord your God is with you wherever you go" (ESV).

Isaiah 41:10 "Fear not, for I am with you; be not dismayed, for I am your God; I will strengthen you, I will help you, I will uphold you with my righteous right hand" (NKJV).

---

[7] Xochitl Dixon. Our Daily Bread Ministries. Zondervan

I have experienced many hardships in my life, and each time I tell myself that the experience is so unbearable, I felt that I have experienced every possible hardship under the sun. at least, so I thought. I have experienced the loss of loved ones before, but never experienced the loss of a child. As result,I loss track of the days of the week, no idea when it's morning or night. It was as if I lost touch with reality and I did not even care. What I endured was the worst pain of all. But the beautiful thing about this experience is that I am praising my way through. Not doing it alone, and doing it with my Savior, is the most beautiful experience ever. One may ask how can I experience the loss of my child and say that the experience is beautiful. I won't tell you that I am not suffering, nor am I saying that it doesn't hurt. I won't sit here trying to explain it, simply because I cannot. All that I can say is that God is amazing. My relationship with God is so unique and special that there are no words in the vocabulary to describe it. I am going through but at the same time I'm not going through, does it make sense? God is awesome and when invited, He gladly stands with us and comforts us.

Yvonne Davis-Weir

The Bible tells of many of God's disciples who experienced great pain in their lives, yet they stood tall and bore their pain with great strength and pride. Despite the fact that they did not understand the reason for their suffering, they continued to praise and trust in God. It is not quite clear whether Job knew the full details of his suffering, nor is it clear whether he knew that Satan was after his life, or how God bragged about him, but he trusted God enough to suffer through. There are other stories of people whose faith were tested and they persevered. These stories are both inspirational and realistic. They are similar to the issues we are facing today.

"The Bible does not promise that suffering will issue full resolution or a happy 'ending' in this life. But these stories show how people of faith have dealt with the variety of suffering and walked through the furnace with God's help. These stories remind us to recognize God's presence even in the worst of times. Especially in the worst of times." [8]

During my time of grieving, I began to understand

---

[8] Timothy Keller. Walking With God Through Pain and Suffering. Riverhead Books. New York, NY.

that even though the pain is so intense, that God is strengthening me day by day. There were many times I believed that I couldn't make it through the next minute, but with the Holy Spirit as my source, I was able to endure. Therefore it is my duty to praise Him because He was my constant companion during my darkest hours and beyond, and He certainly is with me today. When someone is constantly thinking about you and your well-being even when you are not thinking about them, it has to be the most sincere kind of love. Since we are given the free will to praise and worship whoever or whatever we wish, I proudly made the decision to choose good, by choosing God.

Praising God in our pain is never easy. It is very difficult to think about anything else than what you are currently experiencing. Each day spent in pain makes it more difficult to get out of our pain-mode. So, asking God for guidance even in our pain and suffering will make the experience more bearable and endurable. According to Nancy "Do you know what it is like to groan with sorrows? Part of being human is that when you lose something or someone that is valuable to you, you agonize over that loss, and there is nothing wrong with that. Your tears do not reflect a lack of faith"[9]

The minute we make the attempt to rise above it, we will begin to see positive changes. It is very important for us to not dwell in that mode, but to make every effort to rise above it, as painful as it may be.

"The power of praise lifted my life beyond the misery. Transcending my earthly reality, it called my redeemed heart to all that is eternally true for the child of God. In ways I did not understand at the time, but have come to appreciate praise turned my love to worship" [10] During my mourning, I realized that every effort I made to put my thoughts on the things of God, then I began to see changes. I thank God that I know Him because on my own I could not make it. The same applies to everyone, we all need Jesus. "Our lives can be painful at times, yet praising God out of the midst

---

[9] Nancy Guthrie. Tynsdale House Publishers, Inc. Wheaton, IL.

[10] Ed Underwood. Praising God in the Midst of Misery.

of the pain, as sacrificial as it may be, puts you in the position of an overcomer." [11]

I can never forget the story of Abraham, his courage and how he pressed on to do God's work even though he was hurting. The Bible said that the Lord told Abraham to offer his son as a sacrifice. The son who was promised to this godly man and his wife Sarah. The son who was given to them in their old age. The son who was promised to them to be the heir, to carry on the legacy. Sound confusing, right? It is possible that Abraham was just as puzzled and confused as we are, yet he obeyed. The Bible described Abraham rising early in the morning, taking his promised heir to offer him as a sacrifice. While reading this story, it is not clear whether Abraham alerted his wife to what he was about to do. I wonder if she would've convinced him not to do it. Only God knows. I was so impressed with Abraham's acts of great faith. Genesis 22:4 states "On the third day Abraham looked up and saw the place in the distance. He said to his servants, "Stay here with the donkey while I and

---

[11] Shane Warren. Unlocking the Heavens: Release the Supernatural Power of Your Worship.

the boy go over there. We will worship and then we will come back to you" (NIV). Abraham described the sacrificing of his son as an act of worshipping. He was in great pain just at the thought of losing his son, yet he was intent on worshipping God. It made me wonder about my faith in God, because after hearing that my son was no longer here with us, my first reaction was to ask "Why God?" I did not think about praising and worshipping at the time. I immediately wanted to know why was he taken away from me. Abraham taught me an important lesson: that even in our pain, we must praise, also that our praise to God must be continuous, in good as well as bad times. From the biblical reading we can only hypothesize Abraham's mindset as he walked with his son to that location. However I can say this, that it wasn't an easy walk. He must have experienced a lot of mixed emotions as he journeyed to the location to sacrifice his son. He probably became depressed, sad, angry, maybe he doubted, and probably questioned God. Who knows? he probably pleaded with God to spare his son, the very son that was promised to him. Yet in spite of all those emotions, he told his men that he was going to worship. Abraham believed in God because he knew who God is and he knew that God is able. He also knew that even if God allowed him to sacrifice his son, that God is capable of restoring or replacing him. Either way, he knew that God has everything under control. His actions also teach us that no matter what we are going through, we just be continuous in our praise.

We praise God in our giving

Many people do not realize that giving our tithes and offering wholeheartedly to the church is also a form of praise. Some of us are faithful in our church attendance, participation in every aspect, be present at every church cook-out, every board meeting, yet unfaithful in our giving. Do you want to know how God feels about our unwillingness to give? Read Malachi 3, which showed God scolding the people for worshipping in some aspects but refusing to do the same in their giving. Surprisingly, they asked "How are we robbing you?" (V.8. NIV). The Lord responded "In tithes and offerings. You are under a curse- your whole nation- because you are robbing me. Bring the whole tithe into the storehouse, that there may be food in my house. Test me in this,' says the Lord Almighty, 'and see if I will not throw open the floodgates of heaven and pour out so much blessing that there will not be room enough to store it" (v. 8-10. NIV). The scripture went on further to say "Then all the nations will call you blessed, for yours will be a delightful land," says the Lord Almighty" (v. 12. NIV).

Since this is a commandment with promise attached, I am inclined to believe that when we bless the church with the giving of our tithes and offering, God will bless us just as promised. This statement is so often misunderstood by so many. The problem is that many are giving and looking for the blessing in certain ways, and when they don't see it in the way that they are looking, then they begin to question God. Some even go as far as stop giving to the church

> Like poverty, prosperity cannot be measured in dollars and cents. There is not enough money in the world that could cause God to consider us wealthy and pleasing in His sight. The only way our prosperity can please God is if it comes through obeying Him. For the

Christian, prosperity is not the attainment of money. It is the fulfillment of God's purpose. This is where the real treasures of God are. He has eternal glory in store for us that will never run out. His supply is everlasting and there is more wealth in His eternal presence than all the gold mines in the world.[12]

As my Pastor Damon Palmer at Lighthouse Christian Fellowship said "Tithing is a form of offering as we are offering praise to God."

---

[12] Niral Russell Burnett. Tithing and Still Broke. Eternal Word Publishing. Irondale, AL.

THREE

THE IMPORTANCE OF OUR PRAISE

But the hour is coming, and is now
here, when the true worshippers
will worship the Father in spirit
and truth, for the Father is seeking
such people. (John 4:23. ESV).

PRAISE IS GIVING HONOR AND THANKS TO THE MOST
High God. It allows us to be on one accord with our
Savior. It puts us in a different frame of mindset, it is
unexplainable. It also put us at peace with others, and

it helps us to become more appreciative. It should take precedence over everything else in our lives. This is why our praise is so important because it helps us to have change-of hearts, and subsequently change our ways of thinking and living. Praising God is simply a beautiful feeling, it is the answer to most of our problems. James 5:13 asks "Is anyone among you in trouble? Let them pray. Is anyone happy? Let them sing songs of praise" (NIV).

When we get into praise and worship-mode, we allow the Holy Spirit to draw near to us. There is no need for us to question the importance and reason for praise, the fact that Jesus died for our sins on the cross is reason enough. It is also important to praise the Almighty because He is our Creator who lovingly and carefully made us in His image. The scripture says "So God created men in his own image, in the image of God he created him, male and female he created them' (Genesis 1:27. ESV). If that is not a demonstration of genuine love, then I don't know what is. He even went a step further to provide a place for us to live. What an awesome God.

We must adapt the Apostle Paul's passion for God, and reason for his praise. He said in Philippians 3:10 "I want to know Christ – yes, to know the power of his resurrection and participation in his sufferings, becoming like him in his death" (NIV). Joseph Carrol states,

> Nothing is more sorely needed in the church today than a renewed emphasis on worship. Sadly, the prevailing winds seem to be blowing exactly the opposite direction. The popular themes in Christian publishing appear to be self-help, self-esteem, self-love, self-fulfillment, self-development and other self-oriented fashions. Even the 'deeper life' literature is tainted with an intense self-focus, promising victory, fulfillment, contentment, and other human-centered goals. Those things are fine, even desirable, but they're the by-product of a life lived for God's glory.[13]

---

[13] Joseph S. Carroll. How to Worship Jesus Christ. Moody Publishers. Chicago, IL.

It is very sad that in today's society many are refusing to give God what is due to Him. This is because they are so distracted with worldly affairs. Too many of these distractions caused them to short-change God. In the end they give Him their left-overs, and sometimes nothing at all. The Bible frowns on their unenthusiastic and lukewarm efforts. Straddling the fence is definitely unacceptable, one has to decide whether it is God or the world.

Revelation 3:15 states "I know your deeds, that you are neither cold nor hot. I wish you were either one or the other" (NIV).

Matthew 16:24 also says "Then Jesus said to his disciples, 'Whoever wants to be my disciple must deny themselves and take up their cross and follow me" (NIV).

Romans 6:11 also states "In the same way, count yourselves dead to sin but alive to God in Christ Jesus" (NIV). It is impossible for us to be devoted to God and man.

Striving to give God our best should be our main goal. He wants all of us or no part of us. He said in Matthew

22:37 "Thou shalt love the Lord thy God with all thy heart, and with all thy soul, and with all thy mind" (KJV). Therefore, we can show our love for our Savior by praising Him wholeheartedly.

Our praise is also important because it helps to improve our lifestyles., not only spiritually but physically as well. Having the power of praise helps us to live stress-free lives, which aids us in normalizing our blood pressure. When our blood pressure is stabilized, our hearts will function at their normal rates. With normal-beating hearts, we will have the strength and stamina to praise and worship. It is good for our well-being, and also free and natural. As a result of our normal body functions, our overall relationship with God will likely to be improved.

> In fact, to forget to praise God is to refuse to benefit ourselves, for praise, like prayer, is one of the greatest means of fostering spiritual growth. Praise help lift our burdens, strengthen our hope, and increase out faith. It is a healthy, invigorating exercise that quickens the

> pulse of believers, prepare us for new
> ventures in our Master's service. [14]

Another great importance of our praise is the fact that it keeps the devil away. The scripture states "Submit yourselves therefore to God. Resist the devil, and he will flee from you" (James 4:8, KJV). When the Bible says we must resist the devil, it is not implying that we should do this on our own in our own strength, because that will be a losing effort. Therefore, since we need the Holy Spirit for this battle, we must use our praise to God in order to combat that mysterious fallen angel. We do so by first humbling ourselves before the Lord, listen to His instructions and be prepared to fight for our lives. It is important to walk with God because the devil is sly enough to notice when we are spiritually tired and about to give up. So aligning our lives according to God's leading is vital for winning and surviving in this life. I'm almost certain that the devil will not waste his time hanging around someone who praises God wholeheartedly and continually. He will certainly think twice before approaching

[14] Jim Reimann. Morning by Morning: the Devotions of Charles Spurgeon. Zondervan. Grand Rapids, MI.

a spiritually charged man or woman of God. The scripture instructs us to "Rejoice always pray without ceasing, give thanks in all circumstances, for this is the will of God in Christ Jesus for you" (1 Thessalonians 5: 16-18, ESV). One may ask, 'How can someone pray without ceasing?'. Revelation 5:13 describes the scene in heaven "And every created thing which is in heaven and on the earth and under the earth and in the sea, and all things in them. I heard saying 'To Him who sits on the throne, and to the Lamb, be blessing and honor and glory and dominion forever and ever" When we sit and think about the things that God did, and is still doing for us, it will make us want to worship Him with all our heart. When our praise and worship become habitual, we keep our hearts well tuned and maintained spiritually. The Word of God clearly tells us to rejoice always, pray without ceasing, and in everything give thanks.

FOUR

WHY DOES GOD REQUIRE OUR PRAISE?

"Praise the Lord! Praise God in
His sanctuary; Praise Him in His
mighty firmament! Praise Him
in His mighty acts; Praise Him
according to His excellent greatness."
Psalm 150:1-2 (NKJV).

I BELIEVE THAT OUR GOD IS SO GREAT AND AWESOME that the best way to honor Him is to offer our praise. He is the Creator of our lives, as well as of this world, so obviously He alone deserves our praise. All the money in the world is not enough to compensate for His goodness towards us. Therefore, since we will never be in the position to negotiate, our praise will suffice. 1 Chronicles 16:25 says "For great is the Lord and greatly to be praised; he also is to be feared above all gods" (KJV). John Piper says "But not only does the pursuit of joy in God gives strength to endure, it is the key to breaking the power of sin on our way to heaven"[15]

The Holy Bible is written with numerous praise chapters and verses for special reasons. As we study God's Word, we are in fact involved in praise and worship. I don't want to give the impression that God is a praised-starved egotistical, self-centered individual who is sitting in heaven demanding us to satisfy His needs through our praise. He could've demanded us to praise Him, however He allowed us to choose. What He wants from us must not be forced, He wants us to worship Him willingly and wholeheartedly. When our praise is forced, it tends to lack the authenticity,

---

[15] John Piper. Desiring God. Multnomah Books, Colorado Springs, CO.

and there is no way that God can bless us. Our God is perfect, He has no defects, no faults, no shortcomings, He's just perfect. Therefore He has no need for our praise. In fact it is the imperfect, flawed ones like us who need Him. Remember that He, and only He alone is worthy of our praise. So it is right for us to praise our God. It is not as if He won't survive without our praise. He wants nothing more than to bless us, so it is important for us to obey Him.

It is all to our benefit to glorify God because when we are not praising Him, we'll be most likely praising someone or something else. When we are focused on Christ, it prevents us from being distracted by the many issues in the world.

For those who have never praised or worshipped God, I am encouraging you to include praise in your daily schedule and you will see the difference it makes in your lives. I am not saying that it will make your problems go away, because it won't. But it will put you into a different mindset. You will no longer feel as if you're alone, and you will have that special peace which will help to strengthen you through your problems. As I mourn the loss of my son, I can feel

God's presence over me guiding me, and as a result, my days are bearable and I have that special peace from God. There is nothing else in this world that I would rather do than praising and worshipping God, who is so worthy. Acts 17:24;25 say

> The God who made the world and everything in it is the Lord of heaven and earth and does not live in temples built by human hands. And he is not served by human hands, as if he needed anything. Rather, he himself gives everyone life and breath and everything else (NIV).

We are the ones who desperately need God rather than the other way around. For me, praising God gives me hope in Him. The psalmist states in Psalm 71:14 "As for me, I will always have hope; I will praise you more and more" (NIV). Let us also read the words in Isaiah chapter 43:6-7 "I will say to the north, 'give them up,' and to the south, 'Do not hold them back.' Bring my sons from afar and my daughters from the ends of the earth. Everyone who is called my name, whom I created for my glory, whom I formed and made" (NIV). All along, God has been molding and shaping us for His glory, nothing else. He doesn't have any tricks up His sleeves.

When we are involved in praise and worship, we should not feel as if we're doing God any favors, or that we're boosting His self-esteem.

> People believe that because the Lord is to be revered, worshiped and praised, the Lord loves reverence, worship and praise for his own sake. In fact, he loves them for our sake, because they bring us into a state of where something divine can flow in and be felt. This is because by these actions, we are removing that focus on self that prevents the inflow and acceptance. The focus on self that is self-love hardens and closes our heart. It is removed by our realization that in our own right we are nothing but what is good comes from the Lord. This yields the softening of the heart and humility from which reverence and worship flow.[16]

[16] Emanuel Swedenborg, Johnathon S. Rose, Reuben P. Bell. Swedenborg's Foundation. Westchester, PA.

As believers, let us not go into this wonderful relationship with the 'what's in it for me' mentality. Enter wholeheartedly knowing that our Heavenly Father loves us unconditionally, and therefore every bit of our praise is due to Him.

FIVE

WHO ARE REQUIRED TO PRAISE GOD?

*"Let everything that hath breath praise
the Lord" Psalm 150:6. (KJV).*

NEHEMIAH 9:6 SAYS "YOU ARE THE LORD, YOU ALONE. You have made the heaven of heavens, with all their host, the earth and all that is on it, the seas and all that is in them; and You preserve all of them; and the most high of heaven worships you" (ESV). The scripture says everything that is breathing must praise God. Therefore, since animals are breathing beings, they too are required to praise God. Living creatures are recorded in the Bible as praising God. Revelation 4:8-9 say "Each of the four living creatures had six wings and was covered with eyes all around, even under its wings. Day and night they never stop saying: 'Holy, holy, holy is the Lord God Almighty, who was, and is, and is to come" (NIV).

From the beginning of time, God included **animals** in His plans. He created them with their beautiful colors, shapes and sizes, and even involved them in His covenant with Noah. "You are to bring into the ark two of all living creatures, male and female, to keep them alive with you. Two of every kind of bird, of every kind of animal and of every kind of creature that moves along the ground will come to you to be kept alive" (Genesis 6:19-20. NIV). I believe that in addition to creating these wonderful animals for food source, our Heavenly Father also created them to praise Him. According to Revelation 5:13 "Then I heard every creature in heaven and on earth and under the earth and on the sea, and all that is in them, saying: "To him who sits on the throne and to the Lamb be praise and honor and glory and power, for ever and ever" (NIV).

In additional to the animals, **angels** are required to offer praise to God. The Bible vividly describes different scenes in heaven of angels ministering to God in worship. "All the angels were standing around the throne and around the elders and the four living creatures. They fell down on their faces before the throne and worshiped God saying 'Amen! Praise and glory and wisdom and thanks and honor and power and strength be to our God for ever and ever. Amen" (Revelation 7:11-12. NIV).

God also uses His angels to communicate with us in many different ways, wherever we are, at any time, whether we are home by ourselves, at work or in the church. They are true worshippers, and sometimes they worship among us as well. I recalled during one of our Sunday services, I selected a song from the hymnal for us to sing. Not everyone in the congregation knew the song, but I decided that we would sing it anyway. I started singing and my mom followed, then my daughter joined as soon as she got the hang of it. I knew it was going to be difficult but I've always encouraged them to learn new songs. Although we had a rough start, by the time we got to the second or third verses, I had my eyes closed, and to my surprise I suddenly heard us singing in such sweet harmony. It sounded as if the church was instantaneously filled with people singing. It sounded so melodious that I was certain that we were not alone. I decided to remain standing with my eyes closed because everything sounded so wonderful; I was afraid that if I opened my eyes the moment would pass. However, after I opened my eyes, there was no one else singing other than us, but the music was heavenly, out of this world. We were all staring at each other in amazement, because we all experienced the same thing. I felt so honored to know that angels found us worthy to come in and worship with us. Without alarming anyone, we finished singing and, without saying a word about the supernatural event of the morning, I proceeded with the service. However before I could proceed, everyone began to talk about the experience. I was so happy because I was able to prove that I wasn't just 'hearing' things.

Angels love the Lord, and they're always in worship mode, certainly we are expected to follow suit and bow down and worship Him. When we bow down before Him, we're displaying publicly that we are humbling ourselves before an Almighty God.

In Genesis18, the angel of the Lord visited Abraham and Sarah to give them the Good News, the story described Joseph falling to his feet in worship (Genesis 18:1-2. NIV). The angels were created to worship God, and so are we. In Hebrew 13:2, Paul cautioned us about the importance of entertaining strangers among us, because we are sometimes entertaining angels unaware.

However, we must, on the other hand be discerning in recognizing holy angels in contrast to demonic angels. Satan in his evil ways can be very cunning. I am not praising him in any way, I am just issuing a word of caution about his devious ways. 2 Corinthians 11:14 says "And no marvel; for Satan himself is transformed into an angel of light" (KJV). Dr. David Jeremiah states "The devil can ensnare us as much through 'angelism' as he can through materialism or sexual lust or power hunger. In fact he has scored some of the greatest triumphs in the disguise of angels" [17]

---

[17] David Jeremiah. Angels: Who They Are and How They Help. Multinomah Books. Colorado Springs. Colorado.

Nations are required to praise God as well. Psalm 67:4 says "Let the nations be glad and sing for joy" (ESV). Psalm 33:12 also states "Blessed be the nation whose God is the Lord" (ESV).

According to the scriptures, It is God's desire for all nations to worship Him. "God is infinitely passionate for his glory and for its praise among the nations. He has been, is now, and always will be supreme in missions, until the Lord Jesus himself returns and brings history as we know it to a close." [18]

Even though God wants the nation to praise Him, in this age, many nations are falling away from the faith. Many of our churches today are so sophistically constructed with much focus on state of the art technologies that the reverence to God takes second place. All of this is supposed to enhance worship, and subsequently minister to the masses. All of this sounds very good, but the question is 'Who gets the glory?' I must be clear in stating that I am not speaking against the different kinds of worship, as each church's preference will more than likely be different. The

[18] John Piper. Let the Nations Be Glad: The Supremacy of God in Missions. Baker Academic. Grand Rapids, MI.

point I am trying to make is that no matter what our praising methods are, all our praises must be solely directed to our Almighty God.

Many nations are falling away from the true gospel and leaning towards the worldly styles of worship, for different reasons. Nevertheless, the scripture says "That, at the name of Jesus every knee shall bow of things in heaven, and things in earth and things under the earth, and that every tongue should confess that Jesus Christ is Lord, to the glory of God, the Father" (Philippians 2:10-11. KJV). 1 Corinthians 16:26 also states "For all the gods of the nations are idols, but the Lord made the heavens" (NIV).

Children are required, and are also encouraged to praise God. Proverbs 22:6 states "Start children off on the way they should go, and even when they are old, they will not turn from it" (NIV). When we teach our children the importance of praise and worship, when they are young, there is the greater chance that they will carry the lessons learned into adulthood. This will allow them to be able to share their faith with the world. There will always be the possibility of some going contrary to their teachings, however the lessons they learned will still be instilled in them. We should never underestimate how much information our children's brain can absorb, and store over long periods of time. At the time of writing this book, I am sixty years old, and there are many biblical scriptures and stories that I can remember from my Sunday school days. As a matter of fact they were very helpful during my studies for my degrees. I remember in one of my classes, one of the assignments was to memorize the sixty-six books of the Bible. I was also able to recite from memory many of the Psalms, and even sing them in songs as I was taught. I had no problem with these scriptures because I remembered them from my youth. I say this to show you how important it is to teach our young people. I thank God for my beautiful, blessed mom who took the time to ensure that my sisters and myself attended Sunday School every Sunday. I am living proof that early learning has great benefits.

One advantage in teaching them how to praise is that they will be able to use their weapon of praise to fight spiritual battles. I believe that the enemy takes pleasure in attacking our young people every chance he gets. He will use all his enticing tools to lure our young people into his web of deceit. So we must tell them about God and His goodness, pray with them and for them, and encourage them to become involved in praise and worship. We must teach them how to be spiritually connected to God, and how to become associated with people of faith who will inspire and motivate them. The scripture says "Through the praise of children and infants, you have established a stronghold against your enemies, to silence the foe and the avenger" (Psalm 8:2. NIV) "Being aware of the culture, knowing what other children are facing in their future is paramount for us as we work to teach them about God and His great big world." [19]

Whether we choose to believe this or not, but **trees** are required to praise God as well. I am speaking this from my personal experience, that they too sing praises, and loudly. not even caring whether they are in or out of harmony. Isaiah 55:12 states "You will go out in joy and be led forth in peace, the mountains and hills will burst into song before you and all the trees of the field will clap their hands" (NIV). The thing that

---

[19] Jean Thomason. *Sharing God's Big Love With Little Lives.* Worthy Publishing Group. Franklin, TN.

amazes me about trees is that they don't need to be told when and how to praise, it just comes naturally to them. It does not matter what time of day or the kind of weather, whether there is wind or no wind, God is getting the glory. Even when they are 'standing still' there is such reverence.

A tree stands in an attitude of praise. With arms (branches) uplifted to heaven, it stands in a posture of praise always. When winds and storms come, bending the branches nearly to the ground, as soon as it is physically possible, the tree is in praise posture again. God's Word encourages us to praise the Lord continuously.[20] In Psalm 92:12-15 shows how much God's trees are appreciated.

> The godly grow like a palm tree; they grow high like cedar in Lebanon. Planted in the Lord's house, they grow in the court's of our God. They bear fruit even when they are old; they are filled with vitality and have many leaves. So they proclaim that the Lord, my protector, is jut and never unfair (NET).

[20] Jannah A. Mitchell. Like A Tree Planted. Xulon Press. Maitland, Fl.

So, the next time you are out among the trees, pause for a minute and take a look on how they operate. God did not create them solely to provide shade, to use for firewood, to provide us with oxygen, or to help keep the soil together. They are there to worship the Almighty God, our Creator of heaven and earth.

Many of us are so guilty of limiting our praise. We worship according to how we feel, according to whatever mood we're in when we wake up, we worship depends on how early or late we wake up in the mornings. If we oversleep, then God's praise is omitted from our morning routine. If that pay-raise don't come, or our loved ones are taken away from us, then God gets no praise, instead our praise is replaced with questions such as 'Why God?" or "How could you, God?" etc. We treat God as if He is our buddy. Let's make this clear: He is not the 'big guy' or the 'man upstairs' He is not a god where we can hold him up when things are right with us, and drop Him when our lives are falling apart. He is the Lord of lords, King of kings, our Creator who deserved to be worshipped continually.

One's financial status should have nothing to do with how we praise. The **rich is** also required to give God praise. There are many people of great financial status who believe that they have no need for God because they have everything they need. What they fail to understand is the fact that it is God who make it possible to gain wealth. God provides the wisdom needed in order to gain wealth.

> If you wish to see what happens when we decide to make our riches first-place in our lives, Check out the life of Solomon When it comes down to the end he could only conclude that 'all is vanity and vexation of spirit' (2 v.11). Remember, Solomon knew God and was greatly blessed by Him, yet he turned from the Lord and went his own way.[21]

Being financially stable should be one of the reasons to acknowledge God, because He is the Provider who provides everything for our comfort. According to Luke12:15 "Then he said to them 'Watch out, be on your guard against all kinds of greed; a man's life does not consist in an abundance of his possessions" (NIV).

---

[21] Warren W. Weiersbe. Be Satisfied: OT Commentary, Ecclesiastes. David Cook Publishing. Colorado springs. CO.

In this scripture God looked into man's heart and saw how self-centered we have become. He warned that true satisfaction cannot be found in worldly possessions, but can only be found in Him.

To the world it may seem difficult for a person who is **poor** financially, to worship God with complete sincerity. One may ask 'how can one think about praising and worshipping when one doesn't know where one's next meal is coming from?' or 'How can you tell someone who is suffering financially, to lift their hands in praise?' It is a fact that many Christians who are poor financially have the mindset to praise God. They realize that financial poverty does not mean that they poor spiritually. However the devil tends to put in his appearance during times like these to attempt to sway people's ways of thinking. This is where he uses his cunningness to attempt to kidnap God's people. I don't think he understand how much praise is in the heart of a financially poor but spiritually rich person. It is sweet to watch a financially poor Christian worship God. There are no words to describe that person's sincerity and close attachment to God. They don't worry about the fact that they lack finances. A spiritually charged person does not realize that he or she is poor unless someone brings it to his or her attention. They are so absorbed in their praise because they know that God has everything else covered. Matthew 6:25 states "Therefore I say unto you, take no thought for your life, what ye shall eat, or what ye shall drink; nor yet for your body, what ye shall put on. Is not the life more than meat, and the body more than raiment?" (KJV). "It is easy to praise in the midst of plenty, but praise in the midst of poverty is true sainthood" [22]

---

[22] W. Glyn Evans. Daily With The King. Moody Publishers. Chicago, IL.

SIX

AND IF WE REFUSE TO WORSHIP HIM ...

"But He answered and said to them,
'I tell you that if these should keep
silent, the stones would immediately
cry out" Luke 19:40. NKJV.

IN HIS INFINITE WISDOM, GOD FORESAW OUR
rebellious spirit, as Luke 19:40 states "But He answered
and said to them 'I tell you that if these should keep
silent, the stones would immediately cry out." (NKJV).
Isaiah 55:12 also says "For you shall go out with joy.

And be led out with peace. The mountains and the hills shall break forth into singing before you. And all the trees of the field shall clap their *hands.' (NKJV).*

In addition to the list mentioned in chapter 6, trees are also required to praise the Lord. It is not hard for one to realize trees praise God, and they do it more faithfully and dutifully than some of us. I love to go to the park to do my exercise, and sometimes I would take short breaks. I usually sit down under certain trees and I would watch the leaves and branches from these trees as they gently sway from side to side. They synchronized so well that I sometimes can't help but move to the rhythm as well. Suddenly my flow would seem to be interrupted by the sound of an instrument-type of music. This was an instrument that I was familiar with. In our church, one of the instruments frequently used in our praise and worship was the maracas. It is my mom's instrument of choice. Wherever we fellowship, my mom never left her shaker at home, it was always kept in her handbag. I listened carefully and was stunned to hear how rhythmic the shaker- tree sounded. These are the type of trees that contain little seeds inside the pods. Whenever the seeds become dry, they begin to rattle, and sounding so good making me want to partake. Pretty soon I stopped admiring the other trees and before I know it, I was tapping my feet to the sounds coming from the shaker-trees. I don't know what kind of wind was blowing that day, but the 'music' sounded real good.

In the midst of my excitement, I had to stop because I felt so ashamed that I began to think to myself: God is so awesome and so magnificent that He made even the trees to praise Him. Then I began to check myself by inquiring the ranking of my praise, is it as consistent as that of the trees? or is it only for convenience?. It was at this time that I realized how badly I failed in my praise. I also realized that although God wants us to praise Him, He is not petitioning or beseeching us to praise Him. He gives us the free will to do so. He said if we refused to acknowledge Him, "Let the field be joyful, and all that is therein: then shall all the trees of the wood rejoice" (KJV). I walked away from that experience feeling so inspired. Since then I never let an opportunity passed without praising God for His goodness. I realized how important my praise is, not for God's benefit but for my benefit. From then on, no matter what my circumstances, I will always worship and praise God. Even in the midst of me mourning the death of my son, I can still lift my hands to heaven and praise the Almighty like I've never praised Him before.

"Our world is full of trees. As we gaze upon them, may we be reminded that God has used the trees of the Bible to speak to us today." [23] This makes me realize that God gets His praise, no matter what, by anyway necessary. This goes back to what I said in previous chapter that we don't have to be vocal in our praise to God . Whether we are outspoken, unspoken, or we decide to use sign language, God understands, and He gets and welcome them all. The trees speak languages in their praise that only our Creator can comprehend.

---

[23] Diana Risher. The Trees of the Bible Speaks to Us Today. Xulon Press. Maitlanf FL.

CONCLUSION

Finally, brothers and sisters, rejoice!
Strive for full restoration, encourage one
another, be of one mind, live in peace.
And the God of love and peace be with
you. 2 Corinthians 13:11. NIV.

All God want us to do is to be faithful to Him, this includes faithful praise and worship. What He requires from us is so affordable, in fact it costs us nothing, yet we see it as a burden and therefore not doable. All it starts off with is one sincere praise at a time, and once we get into the habit of praising and worshipping, it will become habitual. When praise become a part of our routine, our souls become inspired and we will be able to motivate ourselves and others. According to Quincy Gardner "When love is manifested in such a way, your love for that special person will continuously be strongly felt within your heart, within your thoughts and no one else is able to possess that place of importance" [24]

I am a praiser and a worshipper, because by doing so I am able to get through each day. As a result, whether my day is good or bad, I am able to cope with whatever comes my way. Praise is very important in one's Christian walk, it is very good for one's health. It helps to decide and define the status of one's good health and well being.

> Take a moment right now. What have you done so far today, do you see all that God has enabled you to do? Starting with waking up this morning, look around you – home, family, work, life, possessions, sight, hearing, love. Can you feel His love in your heart?

---

[24] Quincy Gardner. Knowing Jesus Through Love, Fellowship & Worship. Xulon Press. Maitland, FL.

Thank God and raise praises heavenward, don't wait until the rocks cry out, it is our turn NOW.[25]

Please do not regard me as a strong woman, I am no way as strong as you may think. I operate each day with the Holy Spirit as my constant Companion. Without Him it is impossible. I have many bad days, days so bad that I wonder if, when and how I would get out of it alive. I am writing this book to let you know that you do not have to be fit and strong in order to serve God. In fact this book is intended for all the imperfect people. The ones who realize and accept that they are weak and imperfect and is in need of our Savior. Come to think of it, If we were all perfect people living in a perfect world, then we would not have any need for God. Therefore since we are all weak, broken and imperfect, and we all need Jesus.

I want to share the words of this song written by Charles Wesley, and I am inviting you to get in the habit of praising and worshipping God. Once you start

---

[25] Peggy Edwards. Good Morning Messages. Xulon Press. Maitland, FL.

doing this, I guarantee that you will experience God's power, and you will acquire the need to continue. . .

1. O for a thousand tongues to sing, my great Redeemer's praise, the glories of my God and King, the triumphs of his grace.

2. My gracious Master and my God, assist me to proclaim, to spread thro' all the earth abroad, the honors of your name.

3. Jesus! the name that charms our fears, that bids our sorrows cease, 'tis music in the sinner's ears, 'tis life and health and peace.

4. He breaks the power of canceled sin, he sets the prisoner free; his blood can make the foulest clean, his blood availed for me.

5. To God all glory, praise, and love, be now and ever giver by saints below and saints above, the Church in earth and heaven.

(Charles Wesley).

You may not be experiencing the death of a loved one, your problem could be financial issues, health, addiction or domestic issues, it doesn't matter what you are facing right now. Your pain may be very intense and the doctors probably are unable to help you. I could tell you what to do to ease your pain and discomfort, but I can't. I could suggest so many other earthly alternative, but i certainly cannot, and won't. However I can encourage you to try Jesus. This is the only tried-and-true remedy that is guaranteed to help you. This is so simply because I prove God in so many situations. I encourage you to let 'the joy of the Lord your strength' I won't guarantee you that you will be healed, or that your pain will go away instantaneously or that there will be increase in your finances. Only God knows the outcome of our situations. However I can encourage you to get out of your worry-mode and get into praise-mode and you will begin to see great changes. You may not feel like praying or praising, but if you push your way out of that darkness and into Christ's light, you will feel the urge to continue. The problems may still linger for a little while, but your attitude will definitely change. The change will be so effective that the pain will become bearable. I encourage you to try Jesus now, you have nothing to lose, but a lot to gain.

So my sisters and brothers, let us sing as if our lives depend on it, come to think about it, our lives really depend on it, so let us praise. Praising God on earth does not really rob us of anything, in fact it enhances what we will be doing in our new lives with Christ. So, either way, it's a win for us, because it is preparing us for heaven.

My prayer is that this book with its many hours spent in research will not be published in vain. I pray that all those who read it will be blessed by my testimonies, or after reading some other sections. The most important thing for us all to remember is that our Heavenly Father gets ALL the glory. Be blessed.

"Praise ye the LORD. Praise God in his sanctuary: Praise him in the firmament of his power. Praise him for his mighty acts: Praise him according to his excellent greatness. Praise him with the sound of the trumpet: Praise him with the psaltery and harp. Praise him with the timbrel and dance: Praise him with stringed instruments and organs. Praise him upon the loud cymbals: Praise him upon the high sounding cymbals. Let every thing that hath breath

Praise the LORD. Praise ye the LORD. the LORD."
(Psalm 150:1-6. KJV)

So, the next time you happen to visit the park or you happen to be in the company of trees, and you hear them praising, don't be a spectator, just raise your hands and join them in praise.

MAY GOD BLESS YOU

REFERENCES

Begg, James. *(2011) The Use Of Instruments Of Music. Puritan Publications. Coconut Creek, FL.*

Burnett, Niral Russell. *(2001) Tithing and Still Broke. Eternal Word Publishing. Irondale, AL., Carroll, Joseph S., (2013) How to Worship Jesus Christ. Moody Publishers. Chicago, IL.*

Curry Sr., Rickey L. *(2014) How to Stay Focused on a Christian Journey. Advanced Global Publishing. Shippensburg, PA.*

Dickson, John. Pierce, Chuck D. *(2010) Worship Is In Heaven. Chosen Books. Bloomington, MN.*

Edwards, Peggy. *(2010). Good Morning Messages. Xulon Press. Maitland, FL.*

Evans, W. Glyn. (1989) *Daily With The King*. Moody Publishers. Chicago, IL.

Gardner, Quincy. (2004) *Knowing Jesus Through Love, Fellowship & Worship*. Xulon Press. Maitland, FL.

Jeremiah, David. (2006). *Angels: Who They Are and How They Help*. Multnomah Books, Colorado Springs, Colorado.

Keller, Timothy (2013). *Walking with God Through Pain and Suffering*. Riverhead Books. New York, NY.

Mitchell, Jannah A. (2008). *Like A Tree Planted*. Xulon Press. Maitland, FL.

Mulder, William H.(2008) *Fellowship with God in Spirit & Truth*. Xulon Press.Maitland, FL.

Piper, John (2010) *Let the Nations Be Glad: The Supremacy of God in Missions*. Baker Academic. Grand Rapids, MI.

Piper, John (2011) *Desiring God*. Multnomah Books. Colorado Springs, CO.

Reimon, Jim. (2008) *Morning by Morning: The Devotions of Charles Spurgeon*. Zondervan. Grand Rapids, MI.

Risher, Diana. (2008). *The Trees of the Bible Speaks to Us Today*. Xulon Press. Maitland, FL. Swedenborg, Emanuel,. Rose, Jonathan S., Bell, Reuben P. (2003). *Divine Love and Wisdom*. Swedenborg's Foundation. Westchester, PA.

Thomason, Jean. (2017). *Sharing God's Big Love With Little Lives.* Worthy Publishing Group. Franklin, TN.

Underwood, Ed.

Warren, Shane (2014). *Unlocking the Heavens: Release the Supernatural Power of Your Worship.* Destiny Image Publishers, Inc. Shippensburg. PA.

ABOUT THE AUTHOR

Yvonne Maxine Davis-Weir was born on August 8 to parents Melbourne and Edith Davis in beautiful island of Jamaica. She had 2 brothers Cleve (now deceased), and John, also three sisters Hyacinth (also deceased), Sharon (in Jamaica), and Maureen (Virginia). Both her parents are deceased, her father died in the early eighties after battling a long illness; her mom died in 2020 at the age of 89 from dementia. Yvonne is blessed with six awesome children, they are my first-born Michael who is now deceased, Linval, Sasha, Carlton Jr., Samantha and Clifford.

Yvonne attended Park Hall Primary School, Frankfield High School and Clarendon College in Clarendon, Jamaica. Halfway through nursing school, she migrated to the United States as a wife and mother. After some years, Yvonne was forced to relocate to another part of the county after suffering through years of domestic violence. After receiving another chance to by the Almighty God, she settled down in her new location, she worked as a nurse for several years before being called into the ministry. She obtained her Bachelors (Magna Cum Laude), and her Masters degrees at prestigious Trinity International University in Florida. She became an ordained pastor was heavily involved in the ministry. It is due to her teachings atTIU, coupled with her experiences in the different churches which prompted her to write her first book titled "Spiritual Abuse". From there she was also inspired to write other books titled "A Survivor's Story" and "Please Don't Drop Your Baton".

Yvonne is now close to completing her Doctorate Degree, upon completion, her desire is to concentrate on her company Sister to Sister Empowerment Group LLC which caters to the needs of those affected by domestic violence.

Printed in the United States
by Baker & Taylor Publisher Services